I0768282

Disclaimer

This book is for educational and informational
purposes only. Foraging and consuming wild
plants carry inherent risks. Always identify any
plant with certainty using multiple trusted sources
before touching or consuming it. If you are
unsure—do not eat it.
Nothing in this book is medical advice. Individuals
may have allergies or adverse reactions to plants
and fungi. Consult a qualified professional before
consuming any wild food, especially if you are
pregnant, nursing, taking medications, or have any
health conditions.
Observe all local, state, and federal laws regarding
foraging, harvesting, and land access. The author and
publisher disclaim liability for any loss, injury, or
damage resulting from the use or misuse of the
information herein.
Edition: Second Edition (updated).

Introduction

Table of content:

Teaberry

Edible Plant Categories

Would you survive if you were stranded in the mountains, desert, forest? Growing up in the mountains of Pennsylvania with my family, we learned a lot about what plants were edible and the ones to avoid. I remember walking with my mom through the woods and she would stop and pick small pinkest red, little berries and eat them. I tasted one and it tasted like a minty tea berry, and of course that was what they were called, Tea Berries. This is just one of a plethora of plants available to you for enjoyment or to survive. We learned how to hunt and how to harvest nature's food. The world is full of natural edible food. If ever in a survival situation, knowing what you can eat and what to avoid is important to help keep you alive and to survive. I wanted to provide a short book on nature'.s edible food like plants and berries, nuts and more, compared to wild game, as wild game is a challenging task without a weapon. This book will help you identify what to eat if you are ever in a situation where knowing is surviving.

A. Wild Greens and Flowers

Lamb's Quarters

Wild greens and vegetables constitute a diverse category of edible plants, providing a rich source of essential nutrients and flavors. Examples of wild greens include dandelion, purslane, and lamb's quarters. These plants are not only abundant in the wild but also boast impressive nutritional value. Purslane is rich in omega-3 fatty acids, while lamb's quarters provide a good dose of vitamins A and C.

Foraging for wild greens requires proper identification skills to distinguish between edible and potentially harmful species. Familiarizing oneself with the distinctive features of each plant, such

as leaf shape, color, and growth pattern, is crucial. It is essential to avoid areas with potential
contamination, such as those near roadsides or treated fields. Incorporating these nutrient-packed
wild greens into one's diet can enhance the overall nutritional profile and introduce a variety of
flavors to meals. Certainly, wild greens encompass a variety of plants with distinct
characteristics that make them identifiable and distinguishable. Here are some distinguishing
descriptions for commonly foraged wild greens:

Dandelion (Taraxacum officinale):
Distinguished by its toothed, lobed leaves forming a rosette.
Leaves exude a slightly bitter taste, with a central stem supporting a yellow flower
head when in bloom.
Also great for making wine!

Purslane (Portulaca oleracea):
Characterized by succulent, paddle-shaped leaves with a shiny surface.
Purslane has a crisp texture and a subtle lemony flavor, making it a refreshing
Addition to salads.

Lamb's Quarters (Chenopodium album):
Recognizable by its toothed, diamond-shaped leaves covered in a white powdery
coating.
Leaves have a mild, spinach-like taste, and the plant often reaches a height of one
to four feet.

Chickweed (Stellaria media):
Identified by its small, paired leaves and delicate, branching stems.
Chickweed has a tender, mild flavor and is often used fresh in salads or as a
Garnish.

Nettles (Urtica dioica):
Easily recognizable by serrated leaves and tiny, hair-like structures that can cause
skin irritation.
Despite the stinging hairs, nettles are highly nutritious and can be cooked or
brewed into tea after proper processing.

These descriptions serve as general guidelines, but foragers should always consult reliable field guides and experts to ensure accurate identification.

B. Berries and Fruits

One of the things I remember is harvesting Blackberries. We had a large crop of blackberries near our home. We would gather buckets full. Clean them and freeze them in three cup freezer bags. Mom would make a basic coffee cake and add the blackberries; we ate the cake for breakfast and dessert.

Berries and fruits from wild plants add sweetness and nutritional benefits to foraged meals. Identifying safe varieties is essential to ensure a positive foraging experience. Common examples include blackberries, raspberries, and wild strawberries. These fruits are rich in antioxidants, vitamins, and fiber.

Proper identification is crucial when foraging for wild berries and fruits. Look for distinctive characteristics such as color, size, and leaf patterns. Safety tips include avoiding plants with poisonous look-alikes and ensuring that fruits are ripe before consumption. Foraging in diverse ecosystems, such as forests and meadows, increases the likelihood of finding a variety of edible berries and fruits.

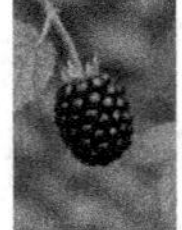

Blackberry: Scientific Name:(Rubus frutico) sus Description: Blackberries are dark purple   to black in color and are composed of multiple smaller drupelets clustered together. They have a sweet and slightly tart flavor. Blackberry plants are thorny and belong to the Rubus genus, which also includes raspberries.

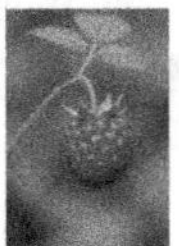

Raspberry: Scientific Name: (Rubus idaeus)
Description: Raspberries are small, red, or sometimes golden berries made up of numerous connected drupelets. They have a sweet and slightly tart taste. Raspberry

plants are typically thorny, but there are also thornless varieties. Raspberries belong to the same Rubus genus as blackberries.

Elderberry: Scientific Name: (Sambucus)
Description: Elderberries are small, dark purple to black berries that grow in clusters on the elder tree. They have a slightly tart taste and are often used in jams, jellies, syrups, and even in medicinal applications. The elderberry plant is also known for its fragrant, umbrella-shaped clusters of white or cream flowers.

Wild Strawberry: Scientific Name: (Fragaria vesca)
Description: Wild strawberries are smaller than cultivated strawberries and are known for their intense flavor. They have a sweet and aromatic taste. The berries are usually red, but some varieties can be yellow or white. Wild strawberries are often found in woodland areas and have trifoliate leaves. They are part of the Fragaria genus.
Each of these berries has its own unique characteristics, flavors, and uses. They are not only enjoyed for their taste but are also used in various culinary dishes, desserts, and beverages. Additionally, some of them, like Elderberry, are known for their potential health benefits.

Foragers should also be aware of toxic berries, like baneberries, and be cautious when identifying unfamiliar species. Here are some general characteristics and information about baneberries:

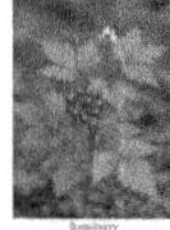

1. **Appearance:** Baneberry plants typically have compound leaves and produce small, white flowers that develop into clusters of bright, glossy berries. The berries are usually red or white and can be quite striking in appearance.

2. **Toxicity: ** Baneberries are known to be toxic, containing substances such as cardiogenic toxins. Ingesting the berries can lead to symptoms such as nausea, vomiting, and in severe cases, more serious health issues. It's important to note that the toxicity varies among species, and some are more potent than others.

C, Nuts and Seeds

Nuts and seeds from wild plants offer a valuable source of healthy fats, proteins, and essential nutrients. Recognizing safe varieties is key to enjoying these nutritious snacks. Common examples include acorns, pine nuts, and sunflower seeds.

Identifying edible nuts and seeds involves understanding the appearance and characteristics of each species. Some nuts may require processing, such as leaching acorns to remove bitter tannins. Black walnuts were my favorite. We would gather up the walnuts until our buckets were full and we carried them back home. Mike would smash them with his feet by jumping on them to remove the green outer layer. We would clean the skin off and throw them into the empty bucket, cover with water and stir, drain and repeat for about four or five times until clean. Dry them for about a week. Once dried we would use a hammer to break them open to remove the meat. Nuts can be found in different habitats, including forests and open fields, and you can yield a variety of nuts and seeds. Learning to harvest and process these wild treasures ensures a sustainable and enjoyable foraging experience. Black walnuts are my favorite and are readily available.

1. Acorns:

- Description: Acorns are the nuts of oak trees, typically encased in a tough, woody shell. The outer shell, or cupule, protects the seed inside. The nut itself is characterized by a smooth, shiny texture and an oval or round shape. Acorns come in various sizes and colors, depending on the oak species.

- Flavor: Acorns have a slightly bitter taste, and they need to be processed to remove tannins, which can be unpleasant. Once processed, they can be ground into flour or roasted to enhance their flavor.

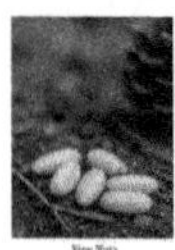
2. Pine Nuts:

- Description: Pine nuts are the edible seeds of pine trees. They are small, elongated, and usually come from the cones of certain pine tree species. The seeds are protected by a hard shell that needs to be removed to access the edible kernel inside.

  Flavor: Pine nuts have a mild, sweet, and buttery flavor. They are often used in various culinary dishes, including salads, pesto, and desserts.

3. Black Walnuts:

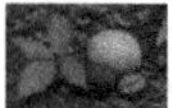

- Description: Black walnuts are the nuts produced by the black walnut tree. The nuts are encased in a hard, thick, and deeply ridged shell. The flavor of black walnuts is strong and distinctive. The nut meat inside is darker in color compared to the more commonly used English walnuts.
- Flavor: Black walnuts have a bold, earthy, and robust flavor. They are often used in baking, ice cream, and various dishes where their intense taste can shine.

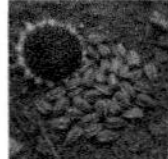

4. Sunflower Seeds:

- Description: Sunflower seeds are the edible seeds of the sunflower plant. The seeds are flat, oval-shaped, and have a hard, black and white striped shell. There are two main types of sunflower seeds: those with the shell (in-shell) and those without (kernel or hulled).
- Flavor: Sunflower seeds have a mild, nutty flavor. They can be eaten raw or roasted and are commonly used as snacks or added to salads, trail mixes, and baked goods.

Each of these nuts and seeds has unique characteristics and can be used in different culinary applications. They also contribute various nutritional benefits, providing essential fats, proteins, and other nutrients depending on the specific type.

D. Roots and Tubers

Roots and tubers from wild plants serve as a starchy and nutritious component of foraged meals. Identifying edible varieties is essential for a safe and rewarding foraging adventure. Examples include wild carrots, burdock roots, and cattail tubers.

Foragers need to develop skills in recognizing the unique features of edible roots and tubers, such as shape, color, and texture. It is crucial to avoid toxic plants that may have similar appearances. Harvesting these underground treasures responsibly ensures the continued growth and availability of these valuable food sources in the wild. Incorporating wild roots and tubers into meals provides a connection to nature's bounty and a diverse array of flavors in the forager's diet.

Expanding the list of examples, we find wild sweet potatoes, which are not only nutritious but also versatile in various culinary applications. Burdock roots, known for their earthy flavor, are used in traditional medicine and culinary dishes. Foragers should be cautious about misidentifying poisonous plants with similar-looking roots, emphasizing thorough knowledge of the specific characteristics of each edible variety.

Let's delve into detailed descriptions of wild carrots, burdock roots, cattail, and wild potatoes:

1. Wild Carrots (Daucus carota):

Appearance: Wild carrots, also known as Queen Anne's Lace, have a slender, taproot that is typically white or pale yellow. The plant itself features finely divided, feathery leaves.

Habitat: They are often found in meadows, along roadsides, and in disturbed areas. Wild carrots thrive in well-drained soils.

Edible Parts: The taproot is the most commonly consumed part. It has a sweet, carroty flavor, but it can be smaller and more fibrous than cultivated carrots.

Uses: Apart from being a food source, wild carrots have been used in traditional medicine for various ailments. The flowers and seeds are also edible, though the latter can be bitter.

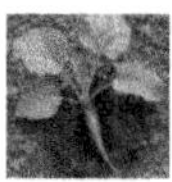 2 .Burdock Roots (Arctium lappa):

Appearance: Burdock is recognized by its large, heart-shaped leaves and the deep, long taproot. The root is brown on the outside with a white, fleshy interior.

Habitat: Burdock is commonly found in fields, along roadsides, and in disturbed areas. It prefers well-drained, loamy soils.

Edible Parts: The young leaves can be eaten as a cooked green, but the primary edible part is the root. Burdock root has a mild, earthy flavor and can be consumed raw, cooked, or pickled.

Uses: In addition to being a food source, burdock has been used in traditional medicine for its potential health benefits. The plant has also been used for its burrs in the creation of Velcro.

 3. Cattail (Typha spp.):

Appearance: Cattails are easily recognizable by their tall, cylindrical, brown flower spikes, often referred to as "sausages." The plant has long, flat, blade-like leaves.

Habitat: Cattails are found in wetlands, marshes, and along the edges of ponds and lakes. They thrive in moist or shallow water conditions.

Edible Parts: Several parts of the cattail are edible. The most commonly consumed part is the rhizome, which is the underground stem. The young shoots and the fluffy seed heads can also be eaten.

Uses: Cattails have been used for various purposes by different cultures. In addition to being a food source, they have been used for making mats, baskets, and even as a material for thatching.

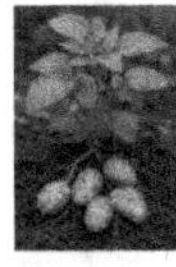

4. Wild Potatoes (Solanum spp.):

Appearance: Wild potatoes belong to the Solanaceae family and can vary in appearance depending on the species. The plants typically have compound leaves and produce underground tubers.

Habitat: Wild potatoes are found in a variety of habitats, from meadows to forested areas. They prefer well-drained soils.

Edible Parts: The tubers of wild potatoes are the main edible part. They can be cooked and eaten, though some wild potato varieties may contain bitter compounds and require proper preparation.

Uses: Wild potatoes are a source of food for both humans and wildlife. They have also been important in the development of cultivated potato varieties.

E. Mushrooms

Some general information on edible mushrooms and descriptions of a few popular varieties. However, it's crucial to note that while many mushrooms are edible and delicious, some can be toxic or even deadly. It's essential to be absolutely certain of the identity of any mushroom before consuming it. If you are not an experienced forager, it's recommended to consult with an expert or rely on store-bought mushrooms. Mushroom is the fleshy, spore-bearing fruiting body of a fungus. Fungi are a separate kingdom of living organisms distinct from plants, animals, and bacteria. Mushrooms come in various shapes, sizes, and colors, and they play essential roles in ecosystems as decomposers, breaking down organic matter.

The visible part of the mushroom, often referred to as the cap and stem, is just the reproductive structure of the fungus. The actual body of the fungus, called the mycelium, consists of thread-like structures called hyphae, which grow in and around the substrate (such as soil or decaying matter).

Mushrooms are a diverse group, with some species being edible and enjoyed as food, while others are toxic or hallucinogenic. It's crucial to be cautious when foraging for wild mushrooms, as some can be poisonous and pose health risks if consumed. Many cultivated mushrooms are also popular in various cuisines around the world, such as the common button mushroom, shiitake, and oyster mushroom..

1. White Button Mushroom (Agaricus bisporus):

- Description: Small to medium-sized with a smooth, white cap and a short stem. They have a mild flavor and a firm texture.
- Usage: Versatile; can be used in salads, soups, stir-fries, and various dishes.

2. Crimini Mushroom (Agaricus bisporus var. cremini):

- Description: Similar to white button mushrooms but darker in color, ranging from light tan to rich brown. They have a firmer texture and a more robust flavor.

- Usage: Suitable for the same applications as white button mushrooms, adding a deeper flavor to dishes.

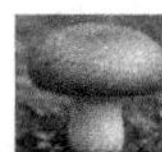

3. Portobello Mushroom (Agaricus bisporus var. portobellus):

- Description: Fully matured crimini mushrooms with a large, flat cap and a meaty texture. The cap can reach up to six inches in diameter.
- Usage: Often grilled or used as a meat substitute in vegetarian dishes due to their hearty texture and umami flavor.

4. Shiitake Mushroom (Lentinula edodes):

- Description: Dark brown with a broad, umbrella-shaped cap and a woody stem. They have a rich, smoky flavor.
- Usage: Widely used in Asian cuisine, they add depth to stir-fries, soups, and various dishes. They can also be dried for prolonged storage.

5. Oyster Mushroom (Pleurotus ostreatus):

- Description: Named for their oyster-shaped cap, these mushrooms come in various colors, including white, pink, yellow, and blue. They have a delicate flavor and a soft texture.
- Usage: Best suited for quick cooking methods like sautéing and are often used in vegetarian and vegan dishes.

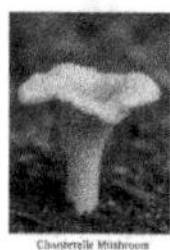
Chanterelle Mushroom

6. Chanterelle Mushroom (Cantharellus spp.):

- Description: Bright orange or yellow, funnel-shaped caps with a mild, fruity aroma. They have a delicate and peppery flavor.
- Usage: Often used in gourmet cooking, sautéed with butter and herbs. They pair well with poultry and are a delicacy in many European cuisines.

Remember, this is just a small selection of edible mushrooms, and there are many more.

Avoiding look-alike plants and safe foraging practices

Avoiding look-alike plants is crucial, especially when foraging or gardening, as some plants may be toxic or harmful. Here are some general tips and information on identifying and distinguishing plants:

Use Field Guides:

- Invest in reputable field guides specific to your region. These guides typically include detailed descriptions, photographs, and illustrations of plants, helping you identify them accurately.

Learn Botanical Characteristics:

- Understand botanical characteristics such as leaf shape, arrangement, flower structure, and growth habit. Knowing these features can help you differentiate between similar-looking plants.

Pay Attention to Growth Habit:

- Observe how plants grow, including their size, shape, and overall appearance. This can be particularly helpful in distinguishing between different species.

Examine Flowers and Fruits:

- Flowers and fruits are often unique to each plant species. Pay attention to their color, shape, size, and arrangement. Some plants may have distinctive features in these reproductive structures.

Take Note of Leaf Characteristics:

- Leaves are often key identifiers. Look at the shape, size, color, texture, and arrangement of leaves. Some plants have unique leaf patterns or markings.

Consider Habitat and Location:

- Plants are often adapted to specific habitats and environments. Take note of where a plant is growing—whether it's in a wetland, forest, or open field. This information can provide clues about its identity.

Smell and Taste (with caution):

- Some plants have distinct smells or tastes that can aid in identification. However, it's essential to exercise caution, as certain plants may be toxic. Only use this method if you are certain of the plant's safety.

Be Aware of Toxic Look-Alikes:

- Some edible plants have toxic counterparts that look similar. Examples include toxic mushrooms that resemble edible ones. Be thorough in your research and be absolutely certain of a plant's identity before consuming it.

Take Photos:

- If you're unsure about a plant's identity, take clear photos from different angles and compare them to reliable sources or consult with experts. Many online plant identification apps can also assist in this regard.

Join Local Plant Identification Groups:

- Connecting with local plant enthusiasts, joining gardening clubs, or participating in online forums can be valuable. Experienced individuals can provide guidance and share their knowledge about local plants.

Remember that accurate identification requires a combination of these methods, and it's always better to err on the side of caution if you are uncertain about a plant's identity.

B. Safe Foraging practices

Safe foraging practices are essential for those who gather wild plants, mushrooms, or other natural resources from the environment. Here are some guidelines to ensure safe foraging:

Education and Identification:

- Know what you're looking for: Be confident in identifying the plants or mushrooms you intend to forage. Use field guides, apps, or seek guidance from experienced foragers.
- Learn about toxic species: Familiarize yourself with poisonous plants or mushrooms that may resemble the ones you are seeking.

Location and Legality:

- Forage in legal areas: Respect private property rights and only forage in areas where it is permitted. National parks and protected areas often have specific regulations regarding foraging.
- Avoid contaminated areas: Stay away from areas with pollution, heavy traffic, or industrial activities, as plants may absorb harmful substances.

Harvesting Ethics:

- Sustainable harvesting: Take only what you need, and avoid overharvesting. Leave enough plants to ensure their continued growth and reproduction.
- Respect wildlife: Be mindful of the habitats you are entering and avoid disturbing wildlife or their habitats.

Timing and Seasonality:

- Seasonal awareness: Understand the life cycle of the plants or mushrooms you are foraging. Harvest during the appropriate season to ensure optimal taste and nutritional value.
- Avoid endangered species: Refrain from foraging rare or endangered plants, as it can contribute to their decline.

Quality and Condition:

- Healthy specimens: Only harvest plants or mushrooms that appear healthy and free from disease or pests.
- Avoid polluted areas: Be cautious of areas where pollution, pesticides, or other contaminants may affect the quality of the foraged items.

Proper Tools:

- Use appropriate tools: Carry the necessary tools for harvesting, such as a knife or scissors. Avoid damaging plants or their surroundings during the process.

Personal Safety:

- Protective gear: Wear appropriate clothing, including gloves and long sleeves, to protect against thorns, poison ivy, or other potential hazards.
- Beware of wildlife: Be aware of potential encounters with wildlife, such as snakes or insects, and take appropriate precautions.

Testing New Species:

- Start with familiar species: If you're new to foraging, begin with well-known and easily identifiable species before trying less common ones.
- Conduct a taste test: When trying a new plant or mushroom, consume only a small amount initially to check for any adverse reactions.

Remember, safety is paramount when foraging. If in doubt about the identity or safety of a plant or mushroom, it's best to consult with experienced foragers, naturalists, or experts before consuming anything from the wild.

Identifying safe water sources and purifying water are crucial skills when you find yourself in the wilderness. Contaminated water can lead to serious illnesses, so it's essential to take precautions. Here are some guidelines:

Identifying Safe Water Sources:

Flowing Water:

- Fast-flowing streams and rivers are generally safer than stagnant water because the flow can help dilute contaminants.

Natural Springs:

- Springs often provide clean water as it comes directly from underground sources.

Rainwater:

- Collecting rainwater can be a safe option if you have a clean container.

Melting Snow or Ice:

- Melted snow or ice from high altitudes is generally safe, but be cautious of pollution in the area.

Animal Tracks:

- Follow animal tracks to find water sources, as animals often lead to water.

Vegetation:

- Green vegetation in a desert or arid environment may indicate the presence of underground water

Water Purification Techniques:

Boiling:

- Boiling water for at least 1-3 minutes (longer at higher altitudes) is a reliable method to kill most pathogens.

Portable Water Filters:

- Carry a portable water filter to remove bacteria, parasites, and other contaminants. These filters are compact and easy to use.

Water Purification Tablets:

- Chemical tablets, like iodine or chlorine, can be used to purify water. Follow the instructions on the product for the correct dosage and waiting time.

UV-C Light Purifiers:

- UV-C light devices are effective at killing bacteria, viruses, and parasites. Ensure your device is designed for water purification.

Improvised Charcoal Filter:

- Create a makeshift filter using layers of cloth, sand, and charcoal to remove larger particles and some impurities.

Solar Disinfection (SODIS):

- Leave clear water in a transparent container in direct sunlight for 6 hours. The sun's UV rays can help kill pathogens.

Distillation:

- Collect water vapor by heating water and then condense it back into liquid form. This method helps remove most impurities.

Clay Pot Filtration:

- Use a clay pot or ceramic filter to remove particles and bacteria. These filters are effective but may not remove viruses.

Remember, it's crucial to assess each situation individually, and if possible, use a combination of methods for added safety. Always prioritize finding the cleanest water source available and then use purification methods to make it safe for consumption.

Many food sources come from water, including a wide variety of aquatic organisms. Here are some common examples:

Fish: Fish is a primary source of protein for many people worldwide. It includes a diverse range of species such as salmon, tuna, cod, tilapia, and more. Fish is rich in omega-3 fatty acids, vitamins, and minerals.

Shellfish: This category includes crustaceans (such as shrimp, crabs, and lobsters) and mollusks (like clams, mussels, and oysters). Shellfish are excellent sources of protein, vitamins, and minerals.

Seaweed: Also known as sea vegetables, seaweeds like nori, kelp, and dulse are rich in vitamins, minerals, and antioxidants. They are commonly used in Asian cuisines and are becoming more popular globally.

Seafood: Besides fish and shellfish, other seafood such as squid, octopus, and cuttlefish are consumed in various parts of the world. These offer a different taste and nutritional profile.

Algae: Some types of algae, like spirulina and chlorella, are edible and considered superfoods due to their high nutritional content, including proteins, vitamins, and minerals.

Water Plants: Some water plants are also used as food sources, such as watercress and spinach water. These plants grow in or near water bodies and are consumed in various cuisines.

Sturgeon Eggs

Caviar: Caviar is a delicacy made from the roe (eggs) of sturgeon; a type of fish found in freshwater and saltwater environments.

Crayfish

Crustaceans: Apart from crabs and shrimp, other crustaceans like crayfish are also consumed in various cultures.

It's important to note that the sustainability and environmental impact of harvesting these resources are crucial considerations. Overfishing and pollution can have detrimental effects on

aquatic ecosystems and the availability of these food sources. Sustainable practices and responsible consumption are increasingly important in ensuring the long-term availability of aquatic food resources.

My family would net a lot of crayfish and cook them just like lobster with Old bay season and a can of beer in a pot. I know these seasonings will not be available in the wild, however for the forager it's a great meal

Extreme Survival food

Insects: In the face of ever-changing climates, environmental challenges, and the imperative for sustainable food sources, the concept of extreme survival has gained prominence. As we navigate a world grappling with resource scarcity and a burgeoning global population, unconventional solutions become essential. One such unconventional but highly effective solution revolves around the age-old practice of consuming insects as a means of sustenance. Embracing the notion that necessity is the mother of innovation, the need to eat bugs has transcended cultural boundaries and is finding its place in the contemporary discourse on sustainable nutrition. In this era of heightened environmental consciousness and a growing demand for resilient food systems, exploring the potential of insects as a viable, nutrient-rich, and ecologically sustainable source of sustenance has become more than a survival strategy—it's a paradigm shift towards a more harmonious coexistence with the planet. This introduction delves into the fascinating world of extreme survival, shedding light on the practicality and importance of incorporating insects into our diets in the quest for a sustainable future.

Edible insects are a rich source of nutrition and have been consumed by various cultures around the world for centuries. They offer a sustainable and environmentally friendly alternative to traditional protein sources like meat and fish. Insects are not only abundant but also require less land, water, and feed to produce, making them a viable solution to global food security challenges.

Here's a detailed description of edible insects:

1. Nutritional Value:

- Protein: Insects are a high-quality source of protein, often containing all essential amino acids needed by the human body.
- Fats: They provide healthy fats, including omega-3 and omega-6 fatty acids.
- Vitamins and Minerals: Insects are rich in vitamins such as B vitamins, iron, zinc, and magnesium.
- Fiber: Some insects contain dietary fiber, aiding in digestion.

2. Environmental Benefits:

- Low Environmental Footprint: Insects require less land, water, and food compared to traditional livestock.
- Reduced Greenhouse Gas Emissions: Insects produce fewer greenhouse gasses than traditional livestock.
- Quick Reproduction: Insects reproduce rapidly, leading to a more efficient production cycle.

3. Types of Edible Insects:

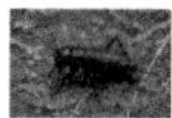 Crickets: Commonly consumed in various forms, including whole, as flour, or in protein bars.

 Mealworms: Larval form of darkling beetles, often used in baking or as a snack.

Grasshopper

Grasshoppers: Popular in some regions, they are high in protein and minerals.

Silkworm

Silkworms: Consumed in many Asian countries, particularly in dishes like fried silkworm pupae.

Ants

Ants: Certain ant species are consumed for their unique flavor, often in chocolate-covered form.

Darkling Beetle

Beetles: Some beetle larvae are consumed, such as rhinoceros beetle larvae in parts of Southeast Asia.

4. Culinary Uses:

- Whole Insects: Insects can be fried, roasted, or sautéed and eaten whole as a crunchy snack or added to dishes.

Insect Flour: Insects are often ground into a fine powder to make flour, which can be used in baking or as an ingredient in various food products.

- Insect Protein Bars: Processed insect protein is used in the production of protein bars and other snacks.

Insect Snacks: Various snacks, such as seasoned and flavored insect-based products, cater to different tastes.

5. Cultural Acceptance:

- Asia, Africa, and Latin America: Many cultures in these regions have a long history of consuming insects and consider them a delicacy.
- Western Countries: There is a growing interest in incorporating insects into Western diets due to their nutritional benefits and sustainability.

6. Challenges:

- Cultural Taboos: Overcoming cultural resistance to the idea of consuming insects can be a challenge in some regions.
- Regulatory Hurdles: Establishing and adhering to food safety and quality standards for insect-based products.
- Scaling Production: Developing efficient and large-scale insect farming methods.

Remember edible insects offer a sustainable and nutritious food source, and as awareness grows, they have the potential to play a crucial role in addressing global food security challenges.

A: Edible trees:

When I was little we would pull leaves off a tree and eat them. My family and I would also pull the roots of some of the saplings and clean them and make tea. Do you know the name of the tree? It is known as a Sassafras tree and the tea tasted great!

Surviving on eating trees can be a last resort in a survival situation when other food sources are scarce or unavailable. While trees are not typically a primary source of nutrition for humans, certain parts of certain trees can provide essential nutrients. Here are some reasons why incorporating trees into your diet may help you survive:

Edible Parts of Trees:

- Some parts of certain trees are edible and can provide valuable nutrients. For example, inner bark, leaves, sap, nuts, and seeds from specific tree species can be consumed.

Rich in Nutrients:

- Certain tree parts, like inner bark and sap, can contain essential nutrients. For instance, birch sap is known for being rich in vitamins and minerals, while pine needles can be a source of vitamin C.

Hydration Source:

- Some trees produce edible fruits, like berries, which can contribute to hydration due to their water content. Additionally, collecting sap from certain trees can provide a drinkable liquid.

Caloric Intake:

- Nuts and seeds from trees, such as acorns or pine nuts, can offer a source of calories and fats. While these may not be as energy dense as other foods, they can contribute to sustaining your energy levels.

Emergency Food Source:

- In a survival scenario, trees can serve as a potential emergency food source when other options are limited or unavailable. Understanding which tree parts are edible and how to prepare them is crucial in this context.

Resource Availability:

- Trees are often widespread in various ecosystems, making them accessible in many wilderness environments. Knowing how to identify and utilize edible parts of trees expands your potential food sources.

It's important to note that relying solely on trees for sustenance is not a long-term or optimal solution. A well-balanced diet typically includes a variety of foods, including proteins, fats, and carbohydrates. In a survival situation, it's essential to supplement tree-based foods with other available resources and, if possible, to seek out more nutritionally diverse options. Additionally, it's crucial to have proper knowledge of edible tree species and how to prepare tree-based foods safely.

Edible Trees:

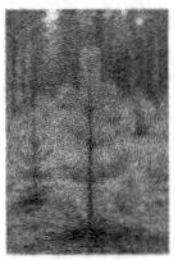

Pine Trees:
Edible Parts: Pine needles can be used to make a vitamin C-rich tea. Pine nuts from certain species are edible.
Preparation: Boil or steep pine needles for tea. Pine nuts can be eaten raw or roasted.

Birch Trees:
Edible Parts: Birch sap is a refreshing drink. Inner bark is edible and can be dried and ground into flour.
Preparation: Collect sap directly from the tree or by tapping. Peel and dry the inner bark before grinding into flour.

Maple Trees:
Edible Parts: Maple sap can be consumed as a drink or processed into syrup. Young leaves are edible.
Preparation: Collect sap by tapping the tree. Boil sap to concentrate the syrup. Eat young leaves raw or cooked.

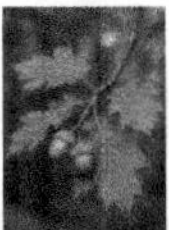

Oak Trees:
Edible Parts: Acorns can be processed into flour after leaching out tannins.
Preparation: Collect acorns, crack and leach them by soaking in water. Dry, grind, and use the flour for baking.

Willow Trees:
Edible Parts: Willow leaves and inner bark are edible.
Preparation: Eat the leaves and inner bark raw or boil them to make a tea.

Conclusion

In conclusion, when stranded in the wilderness, having knowledge of essential survival foods can be a lifesaver. Remembering that the key to survival is a combination of variety and nutrition, it is crucial to include a diverse range of foods in your foraging efforts. From protein-rich insects and small game to plant-based sources such as wild berries, nuts, and edible greens, understanding your surroundings is paramount.

Root vegetables and tubers can provide valuable carbohydrates, while fish and other aquatic life contribute to a well-rounded diet. Additionally, being aware of poisonous plants and avoiding them is just as crucial as identifying edible ones. Gathering, fishing, hunting, and foraging skills are indispensable, as they enable you to adapt to different environments and seasons.

To enhance your chances of survival, consider storing emergency food supplies in your gear, such as energy bars, dried fruits, and nuts. These items can serve as a quick and convenient source of sustenance in dire situations.

Ultimately, survival in the wilderness hinges on a combination of resourcefulness, adaptability, and knowledge. By being well-prepared and informed about the edible resources available in the wild, you increase your chances of not only surviving but also thriving in challenging circumstances.

Embarking on a journey of ongoing learning and practice is a commendable and enriching endeavor. Here are some words of encouragement to keep you motivated:

Embrace the Process: Learning is a journey, not a destination. Enjoy the process of discovery and growth. Each step you take brings you closer to mastery.

Celebrate Progress, Not Perfection: Don't be too hard on yourself. Celebrate small victories along the way. Every bit of progress is a step in the right direction.

Stay Curious: Curiosity is the driving force behind continuous learning. Ask questions, explore new topics, and keep that sense of wonder alive.

Challenge Yourself: Don't be afraid to step out of your comfort zone. Challenges lead to growth. You'll be amazed at what you can achieve when you push your boundaries.

Set Realistic Goals: Break down your learning journey into manageable goals. This makes the process more achievable and allows you to measure your progress effectively.

Create a Routine: Consistency is key. Establish a regular learning routine that works for you. Small, consistent efforts over time yield significant results.

Connect with Others: Join communities, forums, or study groups related to your field of interest. Sharing experiences and learning from others can provide valuable insights and encouragement.

Learn from Setbacks: Mistakes and setbacks are inevitable, but they are also powerful learning opportunities. Analyze what went wrong, adjust your approach, and move forward with newfound knowledge. Did you not recognize the leaves correctly? Always identify before eating.

Visualize Success: Envision yourself reaching your learning goals. Visualization can be a powerful motivator, helping you stay focused on the positive outcomes of your efforts.

Take Breaks: It's essential to rest and recharge. Give yourself breaks to avoid burnout. Sometimes stepping away for a while allows your brain to process and consolidate what you've learned.

Be Patient: Learning takes time. Be patient with yourself as you acquire new skills and knowledge. Remember, the journey is just as important as the destination.

Celebrate Your Passion: Remind yourself why you started this journey in the first place. Cultivate and nurture your passion for learning. It's this passion that will sustain you through challenges.

Remember, every moment spent learning and practicing is an investment in yourself and your future. Keep going—you're on the path to becoming the best version of yourself!

When foraging for wild edibles, it is crucial to accurately identify the plants and ensure they are safe to eat. If you are unsure, it's best to consult with an experienced forager or botanist.In conclusion, foraging for wild plants offers a diverse array of edible categories, each contributing unique flavors and essential nutrients to a forager's diet. From wild greens to berries, nuts, seeds, roots, and tubers, the natural world provides a bounty of nutritious and delicious options for those with the knowledge and skills to explore it responsibly.

9 798877 721821